THE FALLING AWAY

FREDRIC A. HUSSEY

$13.99

THE FALLING AWAY

THIS BOOK
IS
DEDICATED TO A NATION
IN
SPIRITUAL DECLINE

CONTENTS

INTRODUCTION

There is a persistent opinion, within many circles of the Church, that we are living in the "last days"; "the end times". I believe this is true.

I've written the following pages to explore this point of view and to examine this belief from a spiritual, scriptural, logical, interpretive, and definitive angle.

It is my intention to use the central topic of "Falling Away" to illustrate this belief, and I hope that the readers are blessed and enlightened by this book.

"And Jesus came and spake unto them, saying, all power is given unto me in heaven and in earth.

Go ye therefore, and teach all nations, baptizing them in the name of the Father, and of the Son, and of the Holy Ghost:

Teaching them to observe all things whatsoever I have commanded you: and, lo, I am with you alway, even unto the end of the world. Amen."

Mt.28:18-20 (KJV)

There is still much work to be done. As long as there are souls still lost we cannot allow ourselves to fall into a bog of complacency; thus disabling us from the primary task at hand; leading souls to Jesus.

Since we are in the last days we should not be dropping back to punt. We should be pressing forward to score, for in the game of spiritual football there is no gain by turning the ball over to the opposing team.

In the following pages you will see references to scripture. It is essential that you read these scriptures as you come upon them, for no other writings can supersede that of "The Word of God".

I can write no commentary that would enhance the understanding of the "Truth" and be greater than "The Word of God", for it is the Holy Spirit within you; the believer; that defines "Truth" as it feeds you in your spiritual growth. It is more important to read the scripture references than it is to read my words; for I am a mere man but the references are the "Voice of God".

"Which things also we speak, not in the words which man's wisdom teacheth, but which the Holy Ghost teacheth; comparing spiritual things with spiritual."
I Cor. 2:13 (KJV)

I think to myself: "What purpose is there for me to write anything since all things are already declared in the Word! His

Word is sufficient! His Word is full! His Word is complete! His Word is established!"; but then I remember: I feel a need to express what I understand and observe.

We are in the "beginning of sorrows".

"Let no man deceive you by any means: for that day shall not come, except there come a falling away first, and that man of sin be revealed, the son of perdition."
II Thes. 2:3 (KJV)

And Jesus answered and said unto them, Take heed that no man deceive you.

For many shall come in my name, saying, I am Christ; and shall deceive many.

And ye shall hear of wars and rumors of wars: see that ye be not troubled: for all these things must come to pass, but the end is not yet.

For nation shall rise against nation, and kingdom against kingdom: and there shall be famines, and pestilences, and earthquakes, in divers places.

All these are the beginning of sorrows.

Then shall they deliver you up to be afflicted, and shall kill you: and you shall be hated of all nations for my name's sake.

And then shall many be offended, and shall betray one another, and shall hate one another.

And many false prophets shall arise, and shall deceive many.

And because iniquity shall abound, the love of many shall wax cold.

But he that shall endure unto the end, the same shall be saved.

And this gospel of the kingdom shall be preached in all the world for a witness unto all nations; and then shall the end come.

When ye therefore shall see the abomination of desolation, spoken of by Daniel the prophet, stand in the holy place, (whoso readeth, let him understand:)

Then let them which be in Judea flee into the mountains:

Let him which is on the housetop not come down to take anything out of his house:

Neither let him which is in the field return back to take his clothes.

And woe unto them that are with child, and to them that give suck in those days!

But pray ye that your flight be not in the winter, neither on the sabbath day:

For then shall be the great tribulation, such as was not since the beginning of the world to this time, no, nor ever shall be.

And except those days should be shortened, there should no flesh be saved: but for the elect's sake those days shall be shortened.

Then if any man shall say unto you, Lo, here is Christ, or there; believe it not.

For there shall arise false Christs, and false prophets, and shall show great signs and wonders; insomuch that, if it were possible, they shall deceive the very elect.

Behold, I have told you before.

Wherefore if they shall say unto you, Behold, he is in the desert; go not forth: behold, he is in the secret chambers; believe it not.

For as the lightning cometh out of the east, and shineth even onto the west; so shall also the coming of the Son of man be.

For wheresoever the carcass is, there will the eagles be gathered together.

Immediately after the tribulation of those days shall the sun be darkened, and the moon shall not give her light, and the stars shall fall from heaven, and the powers of the heavens shall be shaken:

And then shall appear the sign of the Son of man in heaven: and then shall all the tribes of the Earth mourn, and they shall see the Son of man coming in the clouds of heaven with power and great glory.

And he shall send his angels with a great sound of a trumpet, and they shall gather together his elect from the four winds, from one end of heaven to the other.

Mt. 24:4-31 (KJV)

THIS IS NO FAIRYTALE

Once upon a time, in a land not so far away, there lived a great king. He loved his subjects, and they loved him. He protected them from the evil kingdoms that surrounded them.

As time progressed his people flourished in all aspects and his kingdom grew great and powerful: waxing strong in knowledge, science, agriculture, technology, military might, and architecture; but not in wisdom.

Then one day, as the nature of man would have it, problems began to arise. Misfortune came to visit in many forms and his once peaceful kingdom fell into chaos. His people began to suffer, and life became difficult. Then a prince from an outland province appeared, offering great promise, and gathered up the king's suffering subjects and persuaded them to go with him; promising deliverance from the misfortune that had befallen them.

Having lost faith in their king, they packed up their things, and they left their kingdom behind for a new land. As they traveled to this distant land, the enticing prince convinced all the other kingdoms to join him and one by one the kingdoms gave in.

When finally, they all reached the prince's realm, they found peace again and began to flourish; but their peace was short lived. The liberties they took for granted were now lost and the promise of prosperity became a lie. They had been deceived. The prince's father, their new king, was an evil man who demanded all to bow and worship him or die by the sword. Millions of subjects were deceived and slaughtered.

When the people of misfortune learned of the deception they rose up as one and killed the evil king and his prince.

Soon after; they lived happily forever after.

Wisdom crieth without; she uttereth her voice in the streets:

She crieth in the chief place of concourse, in the openings of the gates: in the city she uttereth her words, saying,

How long, ye simple ones, will ye love simplicity? And the scorners delight in their scorning, and fools hate knowledge?

Turn you at my reproof: behold, I will pour out my spirit unto you, I will make known my words onto you.

Because I have called, and ye refused; I have stretched out my hand, and no man regarded;

But ye have set at nought all my council, and would none of my reproof:

I also will laugh at your calamity; I will mock when your fear cometh;

When your fear cometh as desolation, and your destruction cometh as a whirlwind; when distress and anguish cometh upon you.

Then shall they call upon me, but I will not answer; they shall seek me early, but they shall not find me:

For that they hated knowledge, and did not choose the fear of the LORD:

They would none of my council: they despised all my reproof.

Therefore shall they eat of the fruit of their own way, and be filled with their own devices.

For the turning away of the simple shall slay them, and the prosperity of fools shall destroy them.

But whoso harkeneth unto me shall dwell safely, and shall be quiet from fear of evil.

Prov. 1:20-33 (KJV)

CHAPTER 1

FALLING AWAY

"Let no man deceive you by any means: for that day shall not come, except there come a falling away first, and that man of sin be revealed, the son of perdition;"
II Thes. 2:3 (KJV)

II Thes. 2:3 clearly indicates there will occur a falling away of mankind first and then the introduction of the antichrist. Jesus confirms this in His own words in the following verses.

"Then shall they deliver you up to be afflicted, and shall kill you: and you shall be hated of all nations for my name's sake.

And then shall many be offended, and shall betray one another, and shall hate one another.

1

And many false prophets shall rise, and shall deceive many.

And because iniquity shall abound, the love of many shall wax cold.

But he that shall endure unto the end, the same shall be saved.

And this gospel of the kingdom shall be preached in all the world for a witness unto all nations; and then shall the end come.

When ye therefore shall see the abomination of desolation, spoken of by Daniel the prophet, stand in the holy place, (whoso readeth, let him understand:)

Mt. 24:9-15 (KJV)

Verses 9-14 characterize "The Falling Away", and verse 15 is the revealing of the antichrist.

"The Falling Away" is so fascinating because it is a clear indication characterizing mankind's spiritual condition prior to the return of our Lord Jesus Christ.

There are two words that are synonymous with falling away and are used by scholars; neither word can be found in the King James Version.

● apostasy-an abandoning of what one believed in.

● repudiation-to refuse to have anything to do with. To publicly disown or cast off. To deny the validity, authority, and truth of.

Repudiation and apostasy are defined in the following verses.

"Because that, when they knew God, they glorified him not as God, neither were thankful; but became vain in their imaginations, and their foolish heart was darkened.

Professing themselves to be wise, they became fools,

And changed the glory of the uncorruptible God into an image made like to corruptible man, and to birds, and four-footed beasts, and creeping things.

Wherefore God also gave them up to uncleanness through the lust of their own hearts, to dishonor their own bodies between themselves:

Who changed the truth of God into a lie, and worshiped and served the creature more than the Creator, who is blessed forever. Amen.

For this cause God gave them up unto vile affections: for even their women did change the natural use into that which is against nature:

And likewise also the men, leaving the natural use of the woman, burned in their lust one toward another; men with men working that which is unseemly, and receiving in themselves that recompense of their error which was meet.

And even as they did not like to retain God in their knowledge, God gave them over to a reprobate mind, to do those things which are not convenient;

Being filled with all unrighteousness, fornication, wickedness, covetousness, maliciousness; full of envy, murder, debate, deceit, malignity; whisperers,

Backbiters, haters of God, despiteful, proud, boasters, inventors of evil things, disobedient to parents,

Without understanding, covenant breakers, without natural affection, implacable, unmerciful:

Who knowing the judgment of God, that they which commit such things are worthy of death, not only do the same, but have pleasure in them that do them."

Rom. 1:21-32 (KJV)

"And then shall many be offended, and shall betray one another, and shall hate one another."

Mt. 24:10 (KJV)

"For it is impossible for those who were once enlightened, and have tasted of the heavenly gift, and were made partakers of the Holy Ghost,

And have tasted the good word of God, and the powers of the world to come,

If they shall fall away, to renew them again unto repentance; seeing they crucify to themselves the Son of God afresh, and put Him to an open shame."

Heb. 6:4-6 (KJV)

"This know also, that in the last days perilous times shall come.

For men shall be lovers of their own selves, covetous, boasters, proud, blasphemers, disobedient to parents, unthankful, unholy,

Without natural affection, trucebreakers, false accusers, incontinent, fierce, despisers of those that are good,

Traders, heady, high minded, lovers of pleasure more than lovers of God;

Having a form of godliness, but denying the power thereof: from such turn away.

For of this sort are they which creep into houses and lead captive silly women laden with sins, led away with divers lust,

Ever learning, and never able to come to the knowledge of the truth.

Now as Jannes and Jambres withstood Moses, so do these also resist the truth: men of corrupt minds, reprobate concerning the faith.

But they shall proceed no further: for their folly shall be manifest unto all men, as theirs also was."

II Tim. 3:1-9 (KJV)

I firmly believe the Bible is a dictionary unto itself. When I need to bring definition to a word or idea, I find that definition within its pages. Of course, I use Webster's Dictionary, and Strong's Concordance, and even a study Bible to help me along the way, but God's Word is the final authority.

"The proverbs of Solomon the son of David, king of Israel;

To know wisdom and instruction; to perceive the words of understanding;

To receive the instruction of wisdom, justice, and judgment, and equity;

To give subtilty to the simple, to the young man knowledge and discretion.

A wise man will hear, and will increase learning; and a man of understanding shall attain unto wise counsels:

To understand a proverb, and the interpretation; the words of the wise, and their dark sayings."

Prov. 1:1-6. (KJV)

"All scripture is given by inspiration of God, and is profitable for doctrine, for reproof, for correction, for instruction in righteousness:"

II Tim. 3:16. (KJV)

Truth can only be defined by something that is true. Webster helps me bring words into perspective for conversational purposes, but for spiritual purposes it can only be God's word that finalizes my definition.

"Falling Away" appears to be more of a process than an event. It also seems to reflect a present and future tense: where people are, and will be, in the state of spiritual decline: falling.

It's not "fallen", which indicates the falling is complete, past tense.

"Remember therefore from whence thou art fallen, and repent, and do the first works; or else I will come unto thee quickly, and will remove the candlestick out of his place, except thou repent."

Rev. 2:5. (KJV)

This warning to the church of Ephesus indicates their fallen state, the falling process completed. The word usage indicates they are now off course, they have failed, and they have fallen away from a point of origin. They have withdrawn and defected.

Paul defines from whence they have defected from, and Ephesus: being the major city in Asia minor; more than likely received the letter to the Galatians as it made its rounds through the Galatian province.

"Christ is become of no effect unto you, whosoever of you are justified by the law; ye are fallen from grace."

Gal. 5:4. (KJV)

Although the church at Ephesus was showing fortitude against evil, false teachings, and the Nicolaitans; they still succumbed to the teachings of the Greek Jews. The Jews were insistent upon the idea that not only was the soul saved by grace through faith in Christ but also in the keeping of the mosaic law. This exercise in self-righteousness would inevitably bring about spiritual decay, a falling away. Much of the modern-day church worships in this manner.

"We who are Jews by nature, and not sinners of the Gentiles,

Knowing that a man is not justified by the works of the law, but by the faith of Jesus Christ, even we have believed in Jesus Christ, that we might be justified by the faith of Christ, and not by the works of the law: for by the works of the law shall no flesh be justified.

But if, while we seek to be justified by Christ, we ourselves also are found sinners, is therefore Christ the minister of sin? God forbid.

For if I build again the things which I destroyed, I make myself a transgressor.

For I through the law am dead to the law, that I might live unto God.

I am crucified with Christ: nevertheless, I live; yet not I, but Christ liveth in me: and the life which I now live in the flesh I live by faith of the Son of God, who loved me, and gave himself for me.

I do not frustrate the grace of God: for if righteousness come by the law, then Christ is dead in vain."

Gal. 2:15-21. (KJV)

Other factors that plagued the churches in Asia minor were the existence of Hellenists and the infiltration of the

Nicolaitans. These threatened the church with pagan worship and immorality. Hellenism was the existing Greek culture at the time consisting of, philosophy, art, literature, and the worship of various gods. (Mythology). The Nicolaitans infected the church with the idea that since salvation was by grace, and not by works, their conduct did not matter and thus they led unrestrained lives of sexual immorality along with many other worldly practices.

"For there are certain men crept in unawares, who were before of old ordained to this condemnation, ungodly men, turning the grace of our God into lasciviousness, and denying the only Lord God, and our Lord Jesus Christ."
Jude 4 (KJV)

"Woe unto them! For they have gone in the way of Cain, and ran greedily after the error of Balaam for reward, and perished in the gainsaying of Core."
Jude 11 (KJV)

Many churches today, who know of God and worship God, have fallen from grace. They are already in a fallen state and are in the process of leading millions to fall away as they already have. Falling from grace is not the loss of salvation but instead it is falling from the understanding and interpretation of what God's grace is. Grace is what He has lovingly done for us because we cannot do for ourselves: unmerited favor. Our salvation comes through the grace of God which is Christ crucified.

Read Gal. 5:4 again. When man fails to seek righteousness through Jesus his only recourse is to seek it through himself.

"As it is written, there is none righteous, no not one"
Rom. 3:10 (KJV)

Let it be clear that I speak of "man's" church, not Jesus' Church. Jesus' church consists of all souls who live through the righteousness of Jesus by grace through faith. Man's church consists of all souls who live by codes of self-righteousness derived to suit their various lifestyles, satisfying their own desires without consideration to God's righteousness: this church exists outside of Jesus.

"Having a form of godliness, but denying the power thereof: from such turn away."
II Tim. 3:5. (KJV)

Jesus' church consists of all souls who have called upon Him to forgive them of their sins, and have opened their hearts inviting Him in, and thus have received the promise of eternal life; trusting in Him as the Messiah, the Lamb of God who takes away the sins of the world.

"Wherefore, as by one man sin entered into the world, and death by sin; and so death passed upon all men, for that all have sinned:"
Rom. 5:12 (KJV)

"For all have sinned, and come short of the glory of God;"

Rom. 3:23. (KJV)

"For there is not a just man upon earth, that doeth good, and sinneth not."

Eccl. 7:10. (KJV)

"The fool hath said in his heart, There is no God. They are corrupt, they have done abominable works, there is none that doeth good."

The Lord looked down from heaven upon the children of men, to see if there were any that did understand, and seek God.

They are all gone aside, they are all together become filthy; there is none that doeth good, no, not one."

Ps. 14:1-3 (KJV)

"All we like sheep have gone astray; we have turned everyone to his own way; and the LORD hath laid on him the iniquity of us all."

Is. 53:6 (KJV)

"As it is written, there is none righteous, no, not one:

There is none that understandeth, there is none that seeketh after God.

They are all gone out of the way, they are together become unprofitable; there is none that doeth good, no, not one.

Their throat is an open sepulcher; with their tongues they have used deceit; the poison of asps is under their lips:

Whose mouth is full of cursing and bitterness:

Their feet are swift to shed blood:

Destruction and misery are in their ways:

And the way of peace have they not known:

There is no fear of God before their eyes.

Now we know that what things soever the law saith, it saith to them who are under the law: that every mouth may be stopped, and all the world may become guilty before God."

Rom. 3:10-19 (KJV)

Mankind is in a constant state of falling. Everyone is born in a fallen state of sin. The Israelites fell so far from God that God removed them from their land and dispersed them in all directions. In the days of Noah mankind had fallen so far from God that it grieved Him that He had created man.

"And God saw that the wickedness of man was great in the earth, and that every imagination of the thoughts of his heart was only evil continually.

And it repented the LORD that he had made man on the earth, and it grieved him at his heart.

And the LORD said, I will destroy man whom I have created from the face of the earth; both man, and beast, and the creeping thing, and the fowls of the air; for it repenteth me that I have made them."

Gen. 6:5-7 (KJV)

There was no one to be found that worshiped the true, living God other than Noah and his family.

If you read Genesis 6:5-13 you can see the condition the world was in. In particular I think of two words: corrupt and violent. These two characteristics are the product of the heart's condition portrayed in verse 5. These two characteristics are also prevalent in our world today, and they have always characterized man's fallen nature, so they will be evident during the "Falling Away", and probably at a greater degree.

The goodness of Christ prevails against the evil of man, but at the completion of the falling away mankind will have drowned His love by choice, choosing the way of evil over the way of Christ.

Picture a society that rises each day recognizing God as their Creator and worshiping Him in that manner. Now picture this same society; many generations later; rising each day with no awareness of God's existence, and scoffing at even the thought of God, or rising up in utter defiance against Him. A society now living an existence contrary to that of their forefathers.

"Falling Away" is a movement away from a previous position to a new and alternative position. It's the word "away" that defines the "falling". It's not the fact that someone has fallen, but it's the fact that in the process of their falling they have moved away from their original position. Is it possible that they could move back to where they were? Of course! If they are willing! Spiritually speaking, this would constitute repentance. Webster defines repentance as to feel sorry for one's sins so as to change one's ways and one's mind. Repentance is a change of direction because you realize you were going the wrong way.

In this present day we are still living in a time of hope. Christians throughout the world are striving to reach the lost with the truth that Jesus is the one true Saviour for mankind.

"The Lord is not slack concerning his promise, as some men count slackness; but is longsuffering to us-ward, not willing that any should perish, but that all should come to repentance."

II Pet. 3:9 (KJV)

This is the hope for all souls.

But the "Falling Away" in II Thes. 2:3 seems to paint a different picture. Illustrated by Jesus in Matthew 24, the majority of man is consumed in sin. Hate, violence, and corruption create a state of chaos diminishing hope for repentance. Mankind is suffering a full-blown heart attack. This hardening of hearts creates a shift in the spiritual balance, a shift of willingness and allegiance. No longer does the sun rise and set with man praising his Creator, but faith diminishes to a flickering candle as darkness approaches. Men have forgotten how to fear God. Surviving believers in Christ will be sought out and slaughtered by the tens of thousands, and the antichrist will rise and finally be revealed. Rev.13 (KJV). Christ's followers will be thrown into turmoil. Believers must make a stand and die. Non-believers will be exposed and side with evil, betraying their own families to save their own skins, and lose their own souls. Judases of the last days. The lost will become lost even further as deception abounds with hate, and the love of man will shrink away and wither. The faith of the Church will be tested, but those with true faith in Christ will endure and will be saved.

This degree of falling that Jesus describes in Mt. 24, and Paul states in II Thes. 2:3 is on a massive scale. As I read the verses, I gain the impression that the falling away is permanent. In fact, this society has repented in the wrong direction, turning from good to bad instead of bad to good.

Falling away has to begin somewhere. When you're climbing a dry, dusty hill, with a steep incline, it can be slow and difficult. Then when you're some distance up the hill it begins to rain. The dry dirt turns to mud, and you begin to slide. You struggle to maintain balance, but it rains harder, and the ground becomes compromised, and you fall. Now you have no control as you submit to sliding down the hill. You finally reached the bottom but it's not where you started. You have "Fallen Away".

In a society that is in the process of falling away it is important to distinguish an understanding of a Christian falling away: that is one who has received Jesus as their savior into their soul; thus, receiving forgiveness of sin and the hope for eternal life. We would identify this individual as being in a state of backsliding.

A lost soul in a falling state is one who is further falling away from the very belief that God exists, and that salvation comes by way of the cross: of course, there are also those lost by repudiation as discussed earlier. Broad is the path that leads to destruction. Say no more!

"Enter ye in at the straight gate: for wide is the gate, and broad is the way, that leadeth to destruction, and many there be which go in thereat:

Because straight is the gate, and narrow is the way, which leadeth unto life, and few there be that find it."

Mt. 7:13-14 (KJV)

There are lost souls who have hope and there are lost souls who have no hope. Those with hope haven't made a choice yet. They are still wandering, not sure, not understanding, not knowing. Those without hope have made a choice and the choice is one of rejection, where they firmly stand defiant to the truth. They are "Fallen". The wanderers are in the process and will remain there until they make their choice. They don't realize that they must choose before they die. A man is making a choice when he chooses not to choose. A soul will remain lost if it fails to choose Jesus. It remains to be said that for even a hopeless soul, lost in defiance, there is still hope for a change of heart, but as the record shows, the countless millions of lost souls of the past affirm the hopeless condition of many.

"And as it is appointed unto man once to die, but after this the judgment:"
                              Heb. 9:27 (KJV)

Whether backslidden or lost; they are all in a state of falling. The difference is the backslider has the Holy Spirit in his soul; the lost man does not.

The consequences of falling away from God result in certain characteristics and events. Moral decline begins to establish a pattern as sin takes a front seat and God is no longer at the wheel. In the case of the backslider, he has pushed God back into the trunk. As for the lost soul, God is not even in the vehicle. When you push God into the trunk you open your life up to the ways of sin and the consequences sin carries. The evil that stalks mankind takes up residence and begins to materialize through your behavior. Your mind begins to deflect the truth and you allow ideas contrary to God to weigh in as new truths. (Eph. 6:12— KJV): You become deceived by your own mind; believing lies. You begin to withdraw from a Christian environment and begin to seek the company of sin. This spiritual decay begins to materialize in forms of self-destruction, drunkenness, drug abuse, material lust, sexual addiction, perversions and depravity, hate toward those you love, anger, a withdrawal from all that is good, and a consummation of all that is not. Emptiness looms within your tortured soul while confusion storms. Your enemies prevail against you from all directions as you watch your life disintegrate around you bit by bit; day by day; until one day you wake up and you realize the powers that be have woven you into this wicked web. You've fallen into a hole so deep, with little hope of climbing out. So, you settle in for the long run, wearing your hopelessness like a winter coat, holding on with that iron will of yours because you're tough and you can take it. Someday it will all get better; it will be all right, but it never does. As long as God stays in the trunk, you'll remain the devil's punk.

The Lord can provide victory over all these things that defeat you. With God in the trunk, you fall from the privilege of accessing the abilities to achieve these victories.

"But my God shall supply all your need according to his riches in glory by Christ Jesus."
Phil. 4:19 (KJV)

Only God can provide victory over evil in this world, and there are only two paths a soul can follow: the path of sin or the path of Jesus. It is interesting to note that the word "backslider" is not found in the New Testament, but it is used in the Old Testament, as well as "backsliding" and "backslidings".

It is also interesting that "backslidden" does not appear anywhere.

Webster defines "to backslide" as "to slide backwards in a moral or religious enthusiasm, become less virtuous, less pious, etc.". He also accompanies the definition with backslidden which is past tense. Not wishing to sidetrack on the linguistics of this matter I will move on.

Most backslidden Christians do not attend church. Since the Holy Spirit dwells within their hearts, if they were to attend church, it would bring about conviction. They are fully aware of where they used to be and where they are now.

"In whom ye also trusted, after that ye heard the word of truth, the gospel of your salvation: in whom also after that ye believed, ye were sealed with that holy Spirit of promise,"

Eph. 1:13 (KJV)

"Being confident of this very thing, that he which hath begun a good work in you will perform it until the day of Jesus Christ:"

Phil. 1:6 (KJV)

"These things have I written unto you that believe on the name of the Son of God; that ye may know that ye have eternal life, and that ye may believe on the name of the Son of God."

I Jn. 5:13 (KJV)

"For whosoever shall call upon the name of the Lord shall be saved."

Rom. 10:13 (KJV)

"And I give unto them eternal life; and they shall never perish, neither shall any man pluck them out of my hand.

My Father, which gave them me, is greater than all; and no man is able to pluck them out of my Father's hand.

I and my Father are one."

Jn. 10:28-30 (KJV)

Persecution, worldliness, temptation, satanic attack, spiritual weakness, a traumatic event, etc.; can cause a Christian to slide away from the Lord; but at the same time salvation is established in the soul and in heaven and cannot be undone.

"And grieve not the holy Spirit of God, whereby ye are sealed unto the day of redemption."
Eph. 4:30 (KJV)

Just as the good things you do in life cannot provide salvation for your soul, so it is also true that the bad things that you do cannot cause you to lose your salvation. Forgiveness is always there waiting for you.

God will not default on His promise.

It is not the Lord that leaves you but you that strays from Him.

Some Christians backslide for years with God occasionally beckoning them to return. If they repent and seek forgiveness they can return to the fold and will be received with open arms like the lost son.

"Nevertheless I have somewhat against thee, because thou hast left thy first love.

Remember therefore from whence thou art fallen, and repent, and do the first works; or else I will come unto thee quickly, and will remove thy candlestick out of his place, except thou repent."

Rev. 2:4-5 (KJV)

The "Falling Away" is also characterized by a society in an apostate condition. This is a society that has evolved to a fallen state by the withdrawal from God's Truth. They have turned from what they once believed, and now embrace something other than God's Truth, and are contrary to His way.

This is evident in our nation today. Our nation has withdrawn from its Godly roots and thorns of evil have penetrated throughout all our systems of government, into our churches, our neighborhoods, our homes, our souls. Our nation is in the process of "Falling Away "

God chose Israel to be the nation whose bloodline would deliver us the Messiah.

"Now to Abraham and his seed were the promises made. He saith not, And to seeds, as of many; but as of one, and to thy seed, which is Christ."

Gal. 3:16 (KJV)

"And I will make thy seed to multiply as the stars of heaven, and will give unto thy seed all these countries; and in thy seed shall all the nations of the earth be blessed;"

Gen. 26:4 (KJV)

"And in thy seed shall all the nations of the earth be blessed; because thou hast obeyed my voice."

Gen. 22:18 (KJV)

"And so all Israel shall be saved: as it is written, there shall come out of Sion the Deliverer, and shall turn away ungodliness from Jacob:

For this is my covenant unto them, when I shall take away their sins."

Rom. 11:26-27 (KJV)

Through the seed of this nation, we receive redemption, forgiveness, eternal hope, Jesus: the light of the world; for a world living in darkness; the darkness being sin.

"In the beginning was the Word, and the Word was with God, and the Word was God. The same was in the beginning with God.

All things were made by him; and without him was not anything made that was made.

In him was life; and the life was the light of men.

And the light shineth in darkness; and the darkness comprehended it not.

There was a man sent from God, whose name was John.

The same came for a witness, to bear witness of the Light, that all men through him might believe.

He was not that Light, but was sent to bear witness of that Light.

That was the true Light, which lighteth every man that cometh into the world.

He was in the world, and the world was made by him, and the world knew him not.

He came unto his own, and his own received him not.

But as many as received him, to them gave he power to become the sons of God, even to them that believe on his name:"

Jn. 1:1-14 (KJV)

Through generations these chosen people fell away from God and God eventually allowed them to be destroyed. (Jer. 4:1-18 -KJV)

The book of Jeremiah provides us ample testimony of the apostasy of Judah and the consequences. Chapters 1- through 24.

God chose our nation, the United States, to be a lighthouse for the world; to shine the grace and goodness He desires to freely give to all mankind; a light generated by His Holy Spirit through His people.

"But rise, and stand upon thy feet: for I have appeared unto thee for this purpose, to make thee a minister and a witness both of these things which thou hast seen, and of those things in the which I will appear unto thee;

Delivering thee from the people, and from the Gentiles, unto whom now I send thee,

To open their eyes, and to turn them from darkness to light, and from the power of Satan unto God, that they may receive forgiveness of sins, and inheritance among them which are sanctified by faith that is in me."

Acts 26:16-18 (KJV)

Through the generations our leaders have gradually "fallen away" from God's instruction and godlessness has replaced Godliness. In a government elected by the people there is a certain moral obligation owed to its citizens; an obligation to set a standard; a standard we once set by God's influence, but now we fall short of the mark. In our intentions to do what's right we failed to govern the people in such a way as to protect them from themselves. In an attempt to come together in equality, we've become divided through unbridled freedom. We've sunken to new standards of evil that have shattered our moral compass. We've pushed God back into the trunk and now the wolf is in the barn.

By an act of government, we removed God from our schools, but we approve homosexuality and transgenderism. Our children are inheriting unnatural behavior by government authorization.

Our nation is drowning from the consequences of their ungodly choices. The proliferation of sexual depravity, unbridled lust, homosexuality, transgenderism, pedophilia, human trafficking, drug usage, is all reinforced by television, radio, and Internet. Evil is for sale, commercialized, and acceptable. This new normal is nothing short of criminal for certainly you can see that it shames, violates, injures, and destroys.

We crave violence and sex for entertainment. We are a nation undisciplined, a child out of control, and these types of children are in constant trouble. Since there are no parents to govern our behavior, we grow delinquent and will progress to imprisonment or death. Right now, we are on trial for our delinquency; becoming imprisoned by our right to make bad choices: rights we have so callously embraced. The freedom to make choices must be governed responsibly. Within the parameters of these responsibilities lies a moral code laid down by God since the dawn of man. We did well in following this code in the early years of our nation; but now we are lost on a dark path with no moral compass. Again I refer to II Tim. 3:1-9.

"This know also, that in the last days perilous times shall come.

For men shall be lovers of their own selves, covetous, boasters, proud, blasphemers, disobedient to parents, unthankful, unholy,

Without natural affection, trucebreakers, false accusers, incontinent, fierce, despisers of those that are good,

Traitors, heady, highminded, lovers of pleasure more than lovers of God;

Having a form of godliness, but denying the power thereof: from such turn away.

For of this sort are they which creep into houses, and lead captive silly women laden with sins, led away with divers lust,

Ever learning, and never able to come to the knowledge of the truth.

Now as Jannes and Jambres withstood Moses, so do these also resist the truth: men of corrupt minds, reprobate concerning the faith.

But they shall proceed no further: for their folly shall be manifest unto all man, as theirs also was."

II Tim. 3:1-9 (KJV)

It is man's will that allows for the hope that God provides. He chooses to accept Jesus or reject Jesus, and in doing so consequentially chooses the path of God or the path of sin. Clearly this falling away is a mass exodus down the path of sin: as in the days of Noah.

"For as in the days that were before the flood they were eating and drinking, marrying and giving in marriage, until the day that Noah entered into the ark,"
                                        Mt. 24:38 (KJV)

"And God saw that the wickedness of man was great in the earth, and that every imagination of the thoughts of his heart was only evil continually.

And it repented the LORD that he had made man on the earth, and it grieved him at his heart.

And the LORD said, I will destroy man whom I have created from the face of the earth; both man, and beast, and the creeping thing, and the fowls of the air; for it repenteth me that I have made them."
                                        Gen. 6:5-7 (KJV)

"And God looked upon the earth, and, behold, it was corrupt; for all flesh had corrupted his way upon the earth."
                                        Gen. 6:12 (KJV)

So, I can see this pattern in today's society and is it any different from past generations? It's difficult to answer the latter part of that question, but the first part is obvious. Yes, sin is extremely prevalent in today's society. Is the wickedness of man great throughout the world and every imagination of the thoughts of his heart only evil? Is mankind eating and drinking and living merry? Is man drowned in his lusts, denying God as his Creator? Is man loving his own ways and scoffing at God's way? Is man lying to one another and himself? Are his leaders trucebreakers, covetous, unholy, without natural affection, high minded, having a form of godliness but denying the true power of God?

I see mankind as a society of man who for the majority do not know the true living God, but have fashioned their own ideas of godliness to suit themselves. Many of our leaders are liars and deceivers, covetous, satisfying their lusts by deceiving the masses to furnish their wealth. Some are outright scoffers at God. I see men drowning in pleasure while his brothers drown in poverty: men drowning in knowledge, intelligence and technology, and unable to come up for air to breathe the Truth. I see men trapped in a hole they have dug so willingly throughout the ages and are now doing the devil's bidding. I see a "Falling Away" which I fear will grow exceedingly worse as we now set the stage for the setting described so vividly by Jesus in Mt.24:4-15; Mk.14:6-14; Lk.17:22-30 -(KJV)

Although it appears that way; I dare not say for certain that the "Falling Away" has begun; for who am I to declare God's will on this matter, but I can say it certainly seems possible that it is at its early stages. Again I refer to Rom. 1:21-32.

"Because that, when they knew God, they glorified him not as God, neither were thankful; but became vain in their imaginations, and their foolish heart was darkened.
Professing themselves to be wise, they became fools,

And changed the glory of the uncorruptible God into an image made like to corruptible man, and to birds, and four-footed beast, and creeping things.

Wherefore God also gave them up to uncleanness through the lusts of their own hearts, to dishonor their own bodies between themselves:

Who changed the truth of God into a lie, and worshiped and served the creature more than the Creator, who is blessed forever. Amen.

For this cause God gave them up unto vile affections: for even their women did change the natural use into that which is against nature:

And likewise also the men, leaving the natural use of the woman, burned in their lust one toward another; men with men working that which is unseemly, and receiving in themselves that recompense of their error which was meet.

And even as they did not like to retain God in their knowledge, God gave them over to a reprobate mind, to do those things which are not convenient;

Being filled with all unrighteousness, fornication, wickedness, covetousness, maliciousness; full of envy, murder, debate, deceit, malignity; whisperers,

Backbiters, haters of God, despiteful, proud, boasters, inventors of evil things, disobedient to parents,

Without understanding, covenantbreakers, without natural affection, implacable, unmerciful:

Who knowing the judgment of God, that they which commit such things are worthy of death, not only do the same, but have pleasure in them that do them."

Rom. 1:21-32 (KJV)

"But of that day and that hour knoweth no man, no, not the angels which are in heaven, neither of the Son, but the Father."

Mk. 13:32 (KJV)

"But of that day and hour knoweth no man, no, not the angels of heaven, but my Father only."

Mt. 24:36 (KJV)

"And Jesus knew their thoughts, and said unto them, Every kingdom divided against itself is brought to desolation; and every city or house divided against itself shall not stand:"

Mt. 12:25 (KJV)

As for the church, the believers in Christ are carriers of the Truth. If we show opposition amongst ourselves, we give way to doubt, which in time blossoms into non-belief. The compromising of moral opinions surrounding homosexuality; for that matter sexuality in all aspects; contradicts the teachings of our Lord. These are fallen characteristics and Protestant churches are approving them. Same sex marriage, transgenderism, homosexuality, sex outside of marriage: all being accepted in the churches today. This is "Falling Away". These churches have committed a breach of conduct by stoking the wickedness of a nation that is slowly receding into a mire of depravity and supporting sexual deviance of the unnatural form. They are setting the stage for the "Falling Away" as described by Paul in II Tim. 3:1-5

Churches are closing their doors more than ever, and new churches that are opening are filling their pews with contaminated doctrines. Preachers are watering down the Word of God to suit the parishioners.

"For the time will come when they will not endure sound doctrine; but after their own lusts shall they heap to themselves teachers, having itching ears;
And they shall turn away their ears from the truth, and shall be turned unto fables."
II Tim. 4:3-4 (KJV)

If we cannot lead the lost to Jesus because we ourselves have become spiritually dead: if we can no longer lead the lost to the Light because our light is fading, then as the church falls away into apostasy so will all of humanity fall further from grace.

Yes. The divisions within the church today are detrimental to setting the stage for a "Falling Away". Remember the definition of apostasy— an abandoning of what one believed in.

How can we be a testimony to the world for His righteousness when we ourselves are governed by unrighteousness?

So chronologically speaking, where are we in God's timeline concerning the last days? (Mt. 24:36) Well! Who am I to say. I can only observe the signs. I don't know the speed limit and there are no mile markers. (II Peter 3:8) I can guess, and my guess is we are in the beginning stages of a "Falling Away". (Mt. 24:9-15) As bad as I want to see an awakening: and there is always hope for another one: I can't ignore the prevalence of wickedness that has become the norm. My guess is that we are in what Jesus described as the beginning of sorrows: (Mt. 24:8); but I could be wrong. No matter who you are and how knowledgeable you are you cannot interpret the timeline of God. (Mt. 6:34); but he did give us signs and prophecies so we would know when His coming was near, and right now Mt. 24:14 is happening more than ever and verses 9- 13 are happening in countries across the globe.

The Church must remain vigilant and keep the candle bright; for we Christians could wake up tomorrow and our faith could be tested unto death. We could fall into the characterization Jesus gave us in Mt. 24:9-13, and if this happens, we must not "FALL AWAY".

"But he that shall endure unto the end, the same shall be saved."

Mt. 24:13 (KJV)

CHAPTER 2

TRUE or FALSE

"Jesus saith unto him, I am the way, the truth, and the life: no man cometh unto the Father, but by me."
                                            Jn. 14:6 (KJV)

I've heard it said: "I would rather preach truth to an empty church than half truths to one that is full."

Today's generations are fervently striving to redefine truth. Webster defines truth as: "truth is that which is true."

God defines truth in John 14:6 and those Christians who study the word of God know that the totality of the Word is found in Jesus.

"In the beginning was the Word, and the Word was with God, and the Word was God. The same was in the beginning with God.

All things were made by him; and without him was not any thing made that was made.

In him was life; and the life was the light of men.

The light shineth in darkness; and the darkness comprehended it not."

Jn. 1:1-5 (KJV)

"And the Word was made flesh, and dwelt among us, (and we beheld his glory, the glory as of the only begotten of the Father,) full of grace and truth."

Jn. 1:14 (KJV)

This Truth cannot be redefined: it is established forever: it stands on its own for all men to accept it or reject it: it is absolute. Man does not define truth; truth defines man.

Because of man's rejection of the truth, he is forced to create his own truth in his quest to establish purpose; hence he is constantly conjuring new truths out of new ideas to satisfy the great questions of man.

Who am I?

Why am I here?

Where did I come from?

Where am I going?

What is my purpose?

These questions cause man to embark upon a journey for truth. This journey is achieved in one single lifetime. It is the individual's responsibility to find the truth and accept it or reject it. The journey is not the same for everyone. There are those that are fortunate and have guides to direct them down the right path; a path that leads them to that which is true. It is at that point the option of accepting or rejecting comes into play. If the individual rejects the truth, then the rest of his journey becomes a lie. Whether fortunate or unfortunate it is God's desire that all men come to the knowledge of the truth.

"For the Son of man is come to seek and to save that which was lost."

Lk. 19:10 (KJV)

"The Lord is not slack concerning his promise, as some men count slackness; but is longsuffering to us-ward, not willing that any should perish, but that all should come to repentance."

II Pet. 3:9 (KJV)

For those that accept the truth; they can now continue on a truthful journey.

There is an individual who traveled throughout the world exploring the various cultures and their gods. His final conclusion was that truth is whatever you believe. Well, because I know different, I can state that this is simply not true; but if I didn't know different, I would probably agree with that statement. Now stay with me as I complicate things a bit. Keep in mind, truth is not so complicated, and that it is simply truth.

By briefly observing the fact that the various religions and their gods oppose each other in many ways we are impelled to ask the question; "which one is the truth?" The idea of truth is singular; not multiple. Truth cannot conflict within itself or else it will contradict itself by opposing ideas making itself not entirely true and uncertain; thus, nullifying its truthful status; because truth is that which is true not that which is untrue. In fact, that which is untrue we know to be a lie; but also, that which is untrue can be true in the sense that the untruth lies within the realm of absolute truth. For example, you can make the statement; "Yes, it's true. I told a lie."

I was talking with a young man one day and he asked me; "How do you know the truth that you believe is the real truth and these other religions are false? After all, they believe their religion is the truth just as much as you believe yours is. Maybe your religion is false and theirs is true! What if your God you've been worshiping all these years has been a lie, and theirs' has been the truth?"

Well; to cut to the chase. There is only one God who has proved Himself to be the true and only God. All other gods were, and are ideas, created and established by man as a means to establish some truth. These gods have never and will never impact the world or their believers on a level equal to that which the one true God has achieved. In fact, many of these religions have siphoned the root ideologies of the Judeo-Christian God, and have broken away establishing their own religions, and creating gods of their own: meaning various religions today have derived from Judeo-Christian faith. Of course, in doing so they have nullified the true power of God and have reduced Jesus to a mere man. Some have created their own gods in place of the one true God. These gods are figments of the imagination derived to achieve godliness without God. Their false proclamation stems from God's very existence. It's man's attempt to overcome his sinful state through his own righteousness. By pride he will not submit to the simple truth of his sin nature and is insistent to seek another way: to establish his own truth: his own way. Ironically the template he uses originates from that same simple Truth he rejects. Some have created their own gods in place of the one true God, and if you will notice, many of the fundamental characteristics replicate that of Christian characteristics, such as goodness, patience, endurance, generosity, love, self-discipline... etc.

"Having a form of godliness, but denying the power thereof; from such turn away."
II Tim. 3:5 (KJV)

Every one of us has a birth certificate. This certificate authenticates our identity. It certifies that we are who we say we are; that we were born with that name, on that day, at that place. Every so often circumstances demand we present this document to show proof of our identity. Now this document was originated and written or typed by man. Doctors, nurses, and hospital administrators compiled all the information of our birth, and signed off on it, and registered it with the local officials authenticating our identity.

The Bible is the birth certificate of Jesus. This document was originated and written by man declaring Jesus' miraculous birth, miraculous life, miraculous death, and His miraculous resurrection. The authors of the New Testament are those that walked with Jesus and were there just as the doctors and nurses who delivered you were there to authenticate that you are who you say you are. When you produce that certificate to someone, you're hoping they will believe it to be true. All you have is a piece of paper; a certificate to prove that you are who you say you are; written by men. We have the Bible; a collection of books and letters written by men; the difference is that these men wrote under the inspiration of God Himself by way of the Holy Spirit; thus, authenticating that God is who He says, "HE IS".

Now your birth certificate is a document, and you have faith in it as a declaration to your authenticity: you are who it claims you to be. The Bible is also a document and a declaration to Jesus' authenticity: He is who He claims to be. What prevents men from not having faith in one document vs. the other? It is also a certification of His ministry: documented by men who walked with Him. Moreover, it is also a death certificate: documented by men who were there. Not only is it a death certificate, but it is also a resurrection certificate: documented by men who were there. Furthermore, it is not only a certificate of authenticity for Jesus, but it also becomes a certification for believers by faith. A second certificate of birth is established, authenticating a new birth; a spiritual birth.

"In whom also we have obtained an inheritance, being predestinated according to the purpose of him who worketh all things after the counsel of his own will:

That we should be to the praise of his glory, who first trusted in Christ.

In whom ye also trusted, after that ye heard the word of truth, the gospel of your salvation: in whom also after that ye believed, ye were sealed with that holy Spirit of promise,

Which is the earnest of our inheritance until the redemption of the purchased possession, unto the praise of his glory."

Eph. 1:11-14 (KJV)

"There was a man of the Pharisees, named Nicodemus, a ruler of the Jews:

The same came to Jesus by night, and said unto him, Rabbi, we know that thou art a teacher cometh from God: for no man can do these miracles that thou doest, except God be with him.

Jesus answered and said unto him, Verily, verily, I say unto thee, except a man be born again, he cannot see the kingdom of God.

Nicodemus saith unto him, How can a man be born when he is old? can he enter the second time into his mother's womb, and be born?

Jesus answered, Verily, verily, I say unto thee, except a man be born of water and of the Spirit, he cannot enter into the kingdom of God.

That which is born of the flesh is flesh; and that which is born of the Spirit is spirit.

Marvel not that I said unto thee, Ye must be born again.

The wind bloweth where it listeth, and thou hearest the sound thereof, but canst not tell whence it cometh, and whither it goeth: so is everyone that is born of the Spirit."

Jn. 3:1-8 (KJV)

We become born again when we humbly call upon Christ seeking forgiveness of sin. Turning from our sinful ways we yield to the Spirit of God with a sincere, genuine, and penitent heart, which then enters and establishes domain within our soul. It is a spiritual birth. We become new. Our soul was lost in sin but now lives in the Spirit forever. We are born again.

What is the truth?

Truth is the very essence of God; this essence being delivered to us through Jesus Christ, the Messiah; who has born proof to the world that God is who He says He is. This truth; being recorded by the divine inspiration of God's Holy Spirit; is a collection of documents compiled into one book we know as The Holy Bible.

A perfect example of established Truth; absolute in its sovereignty; can be found in Ex. chapter 7. Moses: asking God what He should be called and God answering, "I AM". The miraculous power of God revealed itself through the obedience of Moses when he threw down his staff, and it turned into a serpent, and swallowed up all of the pharaoh's magician's serpents. Their serpents were lies, representing gods derived from their culture; but God, being Truth, swallowed up the lies as it should be and as it is.

Now get ready for this!

There is no lie in the Truth, and God being truth; there is no lie in God. God created all things, and all things are true. It is a man who doubted God, and believed the lie, which led him to his fallen state; that lie generated from the serpent. The lie exists within man and generates from the nature of man: sin. The lie exists within man but not within God, who created man.

Truth is the totality of all things that exist and all things that do not exist, all that was, is, and will be, all that is visible or invisible. All things nonexistent are not true- in a physical sense. They are true in the sense that they can exist within the imagination of man. Such as a lie. A lie being that which is not true because something did not exist or happen. At the same time the lie does exist because it's true that the lie has been told.

The lie is only true in the sense that it has been told.

For example: "yes it's true, I believed the lie", or "yes, it's true, I told a lie". The truth always remains the truth whether you lie about it or not. There is no difference between the truth and that which is true; they are one in the same, and the truth contains the lie. Once the lie is presented it still remains part of the truth. This truth is all that God is and all that He created. The lie is a byproduct of the fallen man. It is absorbed into the truth just as the pharaoh's serpents were devoured by the serpent of God.

(Satan introduced the lie to Adam and Eve in the garden and the lie produced sin and hence it is passed on by birth to all men.)

"Wherefore, as by one man sin entered into the world, and death by sin: and so death passed upon all men, for that all have sinned:"

Rom. 5-12 (KJV)

So why did I go through all that to simply show that the Truth is that which is true, and the lie is that which is not true but is contained by the Truth?

Well because it is "the lie" that becomes a distinguishing characteristic in the "Falling Away".

"And then shall that Wicked be revealed, whom the Lord shall consume with the spirit of his mouth and shall destroy with the brightness of his coming:

Even him, who's coming is after the working of Satan with all power and signs and lying wonders,

And with all deceivableness of unrighteousness in them that perish; because they received not the love of the truth, that they might be saved.

And for this cause God shall send them strong delusion, that they should believe a lie:

That they all might be damned who believed not the truth, but had pleasure in unrighteousness."

II Thes. 2:8-12 (KJV)

Our nation is in the process of "Falling Away" from the Truth. What was once a great nation that worshipped God collectively is now one that wallows in the consequences of straying from God's path. It has begun the descent into the pit of destruction, and it must take notice of its spiritual condition. Like an addict who pushes on in denial of his self-destructive course; our nation has done the same. For the last 70 years we have rushed headlong and recklessly through change; with little consultation with the God we trust. As a result, we now reap the consequences of our actions.

For example, the removal of prayer from our schools denied our cultures spiritual unity, affecting each generation in line. It granted our children the right to believe in what they think is true but denied them the right to believe in what we know is true. In effect, people of all races have been denied the fundamental foundation of Truth, which is to fear God; meaning to respect and affirm His existence. Though our fathers of old weren't perfect; though they made mistakes; they did manage to exercise this one fundamental belief; they recognized God on a daily basis, and they taught their children to do the same. A simple spiritual task, so easy to perform, bringing tremendous results. The removal of prayer from our schools destroyed our social faith and in turn introduced spiritual complacency within our children's souls preventing them from seeking our God in a diligent manner.

These children are now our leaders in responsible positions, and these leaders are leading this present generation down the same path.

"But without faith it is impossible to please him: for he that cometh to God must believe that he is, and that he is a rewarder of them that diligently seek him."

Heb. 11:5 (KJV)

"There is a generation that curseth their father, and doth not bless their mother.

There is a generation that are pure in their own eyes, and yet is not washed from their filthiness.

There is a generation, O how lofty are their eyes! and their eyelids are lifted up.

There is a generation, whose teeth are as swords, and their jaw teeth as knives, to devour the poor from off the earth, and the needy from among men."

Prov. 30:11-14 (KJV)

This course must change. Most do not want to yield to the Truth. Most desperately seek any other alternative answer other than a spiritual one. Most think there must be another way to fix this travesty: like the addict: he won't go to rehab unless he reaches rock-bottom or nearly dies. It is there at the clinic he finds the first love he had forgotten existed; the strength and renewed hope; the spiritual renewal to heal his soul.

Rock bottom for a nation can only bring death and destruction. I cry out to this nation. Admit you are in spiritual decline. The evil you have done will reap the consequences you will soon witness. Your depravity has excelled to the point of no return. God will allow you to reap what you sow. Your only hope is a spiritual awakening: some miraculous recovery of biblical proportions. "With God all things are possible." Mt. 19:26 -(KJV). Without God you are doomed.

The course of man has always been to resist God and only a small percentage of man yields to His presence. This is the battle for Truth: where man decides to believe a lie or believe the Truth. It is a choice made on an individual level and then transcending to a social level. In the "Falling Away" man will fail to side with Truth and will believe the lie. This is the path our nation is choosing now. We are in the beginning stages of a "Great Falling Away". Like the addict, we have injected our souls for the last 70 years with an evil concoction. Daily injections of a massive dosage have rendered us incoherent to our souls. Our nation thrives on a network of media and entertainment which pours out a vile cocktail composed of violence, vulgarity, perversion, drug usage, murder, war, deception, racism, horror, satanic glorification, self-indulgence, sex, and money.

You are what you eat!

Godless men rising to power, making godless decisions, fabricating a godless nation. Wealth and power enable large corporations to dictate immoral policies. The erosion of Truth within the very souls of our people; raising insurmountable partitions; has left us spiritually disconnected as we now teeter on the cliff overlooking a dark fall to the valley below.

What an irony; that a nation, founded on Godly principles, would fall so far as to declare evil men equal to righteous men. We are equal in that we are all sinners in need of a savior.

It's time our leaders set aside their fears and jump down off the fence to side with righteousness. How is it that in our pursuit for truth we cannot come to the Truth? I guess that leaves us like the goldfish in a dirty, clouded, bowl.

Again!
Rom. 1:16-32 (KJV)

CHAPTER 3

THE JUNCTURE OF MAN

As I begin to contemplate the complexity of interpretation by man, I sit here with my Bible open to I Corinthians, chapter 2.

"But as it is written, Eye hath not seen, nor ear heard, neither have entered into the heart of man, the things which God hath prepared for them that love him.

But God hath revealed them unto us by his Spirit: for the Spirit searcheth all things, yea, the deep things of God.

For what man knoweth the things of a man, save the spirit of man which is in him? Even so the things of God knoweth no man, but the Spirit of God.

Now we have received, not the spirit of the world, but the spirit which is of God; that we might know the things that are freely given to us of God.

Which things also we speak, not in the words which man's wisdom teacheth, but which the Holy Ghost teacheth; comparing spiritual things with spiritual."

I Cor. 2:9-13 (KJV)

The Word is known in heaven and is understood. The Word of God seeks to be known by men and in doing so it is interpreted to men through the Holy Spirit so they may understand.

It is not as important for us to interpret the Word as it is for us to listen to the Word. The Word is the Father, the Son, and the Holy Spirit.

The Holy Bible is the most powerful instrument known to man. It is the voice of God, and that voice is communicated to us by way of the divine inspiration of scripture, and then interpreted within us by the Holy Spirit; therefore, we must humbly come before Him in the Spirit seeking guidance to understand His truth.

The Word is established in heaven and earth but needs to be interpreted by us on earth. The Holy Spirit performs this task with divine precision.

At the same time, we are also interpreters; being of freewill; freethinkers. We were created in the image of God: fallen in sin our souls are at stake. It is for us to interpret God's truth so we may once again be rejoined with Him in eternity.

"That your faith should not stand in the wisdom of men, but in the power of God." vs. 5.

"But we speak the wisdom of God in a mystery, even the hidden wisdom, which God ordained before the world unto our glory:". vs. 7.

"For who hath known the mind of the Lord, that he may instruct him? But we have the mind of Christ." vs. 16.

I Cor. 2:5,7,16 (KJV)

"Knowing this first, that no prophecy of the scripture is of any private interpretation.

For the prophecy came not in old time by the will of man: but holy men of God spake as they were moved by the Holy Ghost."

II Pet. 1:20-21 (KJV)

"But the Comforter, which is the Holy Ghost, whom the Father will send in my name, he shall teach you all things, and bring all things to your remembrance, whatsoever I have said unto you."

Jn. 14:26 (KJV)

"Howbeit when he, the Spirit of truth, is come, he will guide you into all truth: for he shall not speak of himself; but whatsoever he shall hear, that shall he speak: and he will show you things to come."

Jn. 16:13 (KJV)

"All scripture is given by inspiration of God, and is profitable for doctrine, for reproof, for correction, for instruction in righteousness:
That the man of God may be perfect, thoroughly furnished unto all good works."

II Tim. 3:16-17 (KJV)

Read John, Chapter 1

Mankind; being born into his sinful condition; having acquired a sinful nature by birth; cannot discern the nature of God; and since he has his own ability to formulate his own ideas: to interpret he is able to construct his own understanding of truth. The Holy Spirit struggles with man to relay the already established Truth by way of the Word of God; striving to guide man in his interpretation.

It is at this juncture the problem of interpretation of God's Word arises; "The Juncture of Man".

Webster's definition of interpretation goes like this.

"The act or result of interpreting. An explanation, meaning, translation, exposition, etc. To interpret. To explain the meaning of, to make it understandable. To have or show one's own understanding of the meaning of."

God is alive. He communicates to us in a spiritual fashion. This communication takes place within our souls. It is here where contact is made, in the soul. This is the terminal of communication which He created and instilled in man from day six, a conduit between man and God.

"And the Lord God formed man of the dust of the ground, and breathed into his nostrils the breath of life; and man became a living soul."
Gen. 2:7 (KJV)

Now man: being one of free will, can make his own choices. He can even choose to recognize his soul or deny its existence.

You can see where this is going!

If you shut your soul out, then you shut out all spiritual communication. If the coms. are shut down you will not receive the message from the dispatcher; you will not hear God and you can never know Him. You can never experience His presence. You are without hope of ever communing with Him at all. It's like unplugging the phone, or removing the batteries, or cutting the powerlines. You cut yourself off from Heaven and have no spiritual pulse. You are spiritually disconnected.

But your soul is still there! Just because you don't recognize it does not enable it to go away. It stays with you from the moment of conception to the moment of physical death. Then it goes to God and He decides whether it will spend eternity with Him or eternity without Him.

So how can a man interpret God's truth when God does not even dwell within him? Well!!! He simply can't; but he can misinterpret it; and mankind has been doing just that since Cain.

Those having placed their faith in Jesus as their savior; thus, allowing the Holy Spirit to dwell within them; are also capable of misinterpretation, and are capable of forming conflicting interpretations.

The sum total of the matter is that man's own will can stand in the way of the Holy Spirit, thus persuading him to draw his own conclusions on God's Truth.

Again, I say, we must humbly come before God in the Spirit, seeking guidance to understand His Truth.

The misinterpretation of God's Word begins with the failing to communicate with God properly.

Such is the case with Cain. Cain did not understand the necessity of humbling himself before his Creator. There was no evidence of a penitent heart; no sorrow for his condition or admission of his fallen state; no sincerity. Cain exemplified disobedience, pride, and arrogance; there was no sacrifice in his heart; evident by the sacrifice he offered.

God demands the shedding of blood for the remission of sin.

"And almost all things are by the law purged with blood; and without shedding of blood is no remission."
Heb. 9:22 (KJV)

Cain's sacrifice alone shows how out of touch he was with God. His sacrifice reveals a colossal misunderstanding, or if you will, a misinterpretation of God's way. This misunderstanding establishes the path for future generations of man to do the same.

Now, on the other hand, Abel was humbled by God's presence, and by faith sprouted respect, humility, obedience and sincerity. He obeyed the law of sacrifice, and the offering came from the heart. He was interpreting the presence of God correctly.

> *"By faith Abel offered unto God a more excellent sacrifice than Cain, by which he obtained witness that he was righteous, God testifying of his gifts: and by it being dead yet speaketh."*
>
> *Heb. 11:14 (KJV)*

Cain becomes angry and murders his brother. Unable to submit to God's will, he "Falls Away".

How is it that some men can come to the knowledge of Truth and others cannot?

I don't know the answer to this question. Some believe those that find Christ are predestined; but then there is the matter of free will; choice: so, then some will choose and some won't. Notice how this has led me to the very subject I am speaking of: interpretation.

Great men of God; by only the blood of Jesus; share various interpretations on various subjects, such as predestination. Though we all tend to incline towards one interpretation or the other, I personally choose to definitively leave the debate alone without argument, marked for illumination upon the day I meet Jesus, when all things shall be revealed. This way I can continue in love; with my brothers and sisters in Christ; without division by conflict. There are times in my life when I've been drawn into arguments over interpretation and later regret the outcome. For those times I am sincerely apologetic, for who knows what blessings we might have gained from each other if we had not become divided.

Phrases like; "It may be possible.": or "I don't know." relieve the pressure of needing to know, and provide harmony amongst each other.

Cain became angry with the Lord over the rejection of his offering and began to openly rebel. The Lord confronted him and convicted him of his sin; but Cain's heart obviously was hardened by pride, and lack of spiritual understanding; so being angry at God he slew Abel to spite the Lord. The consequences of Cain's arrogant and disobedient heart resulted in a "Falling Away". He was driven out from the presence of God.

"And in process of time it came to pass, that Cain brought of the fruit of the ground an offering unto the LORD.

And Abel, he also brought of the firstlings of his flock and of the fat thereof. And the LORD had respect unto Abel and to his offering:

But unto Cain and to his offering he had no respect. And Cain was very wroth, and his countenance fell.

And the LORD said unto Cain, Why art thou wroth? and why is thy countenance fallen?

If thou doest well, shalt thou not be accepted? And if thou doest not well, sin lieth at the door: And unto thee shall be his desire, and thou shalt rule over him.

And Cain talked with Abel his brother: and it came to pass, when they were in the field, that Cain rose up against Abel his brother, and slew him.

And the LORD said unto Cain, where is Able thy brother? And he said, I know not: Am I my brother's keeper?

And he said, What hast thou done? the voice of thy brother's blood crieth unto me from the ground.

And now art thou cursed from the earth, which hath opened her mouth to receive thy brother's blood from the ground;

When thou tillest the ground, it shall not henceforth yield unto thee her strength; a fugitive and a vagabond shalt thou be in the earth.

And Cain said unto the LORD, My punishment is greater than I can bear.

Behold, thou hast driven me out this day from the face of the earth; and from thy face shall I be hid; and I shall be a fugitive and a vagabond in the earth; and it shall come to pass, that everyone that findeth me shall slay me.

And the LORD said unto him, therefore whosoever slayeth Cain, vengeance shall be taken on him sevenfold. And the LORD set a mark upon Cain, lest any finding him should kill him.

And Cain went out from the presence of the LORD, and dwelt in the land of Nod, on the east of Eden."
Gen. 4:3-16 (KJV)

If Cain had only been able to humble himself before the Lord from the start, he might have been able to interpret God's message, and offer up an acceptable sacrifice.

Again! We must humbly come before God, in the Spirit, seeking guidance to understand His Truth.

In communing with God, the sacrifice must come from our hearts out of a humble disposition; sincere in our intent which is to seek His favor and appreciate His love.

If we approach the interpretation of His Word from the perspective of absolute Truth, then we must admit there can only be one true interpretation because truth cannot contradict itself or oppose itself by any view. There can be many interpretations by man, but only one true interpretation from God; and that interpretation is established in heaven.

But we freethinkers; of free will; have continued to form our own opinions as to the meaning of God's Truth. Through the ages these opinions have created opposition in conflict resulting in division around the world. One of these results is the denominations that have formed within the Protestant church.

The Twenty-four Protestant Denominations

Methodism
Lutheranism
Presbyterianism
Anglicanism
Baptists
Evangelicalism
Pentecostal
Calvinism
Continental Reformed Protestantism
United Methodist church
Adventist
Assemblies of God
Southern Baptist Convention
Evangelical Lutheran Church in America
Church of the Nazarene
Episcopal Church
Reformed Church in America
Presbyterian Church in America
Presbyterian Church (USA)
Plymouth Brethen
African Methodist Episcopal Zion Church
Church of England
Wesleyan Church
African Methodist Episcopal Church (AME)

The conflicting points of view created by private interpretation have succeeded in bringing division within the "flock", causing the flock to break off into various groups. This separation limits the worshipping together as one "flock" in unity. At this very moment there are some denominations dividing even further apart.

Ironically the denominations have turned out to be a safety net for the Protestant church. Though its differences in views are vast, the evolution of its denominations has enabled it to survive the ages and carry the one simple message that can save all men: the shed, sacrificial blood of Jesus Christ is sufficient to forgive all sin. This doctrine of atonement is the one common denominator that all 24 denominations can share. Imagine if we all joined together under one roof as one church in unity: we would get nothing done because of the confusion, the arguments, and the chaos caused by our conflicting views of God's truth. This is why we worship and teach separately. It is we men who have created these divisions in our search to understand the whole Truth. In our desperate need for spiritual security, we have chosen ideas of interpretation that suit us best and manufactured further interpretation to support that. What many denominations have failed to fathom is that the Truth is singular, onto itself, therefore there can be no contradiction within it: it is established in heaven and no matter how we may interpret it, it will stay the same. This is why Jesus is the common denominator which bonds all of us who have received him. This Truth cannot and will not change no matter how much man succeeds in misinterpreting it.

Nothing can separate us from the blood of Christ. We are gathered together in His death and resurrection.

"Who is he that condemeth? It is Christ that died, yea rather, that is risen again, who is even at the right hand of God, who also maketh intercession for us.

Who shall separate us from the love of Christ? shall tribulation, or distress, or persecution, or famine, or nakedness, or peril, or sword?

As it is written, For thy sake we are killed all the day long; we are accounted as sheep for the slaughter.

Nay, in all these things we are more than conquerors through him that loved us.

For I am persuaded, that neither death, nor life, nor angels, nor principalities, nor powers, nor things present, nor things to come,

Nor height, nor depth, nor any other creature, shall be able to separate us from the love of God, which is in Christ Jesus our Lord."

Rom. 8:34-39 (KJV)

"And Jesus saith unto him, I am the way, the truth, and the life: no man cometh unto the Father, but by me."

Jn. 14:6 (KJV)

There are a few denominations who have challenged the common denominator by believing it takes more than faith in the blood of Jesus Christ to forgive sin, and more than God's promise to secure salvation. His grace is sufficient.

"For by grace are ye saved through faith; and that not of yourselves: it is the gift of God:
Not of works, lest any man should boast."
Eph. 2:8-9 (KJV)

"In whom ye also trusted that after ye heard the word of truth; the gospel of your salvation; in whom also after that ye believed, ye were sealed with that holy Spirit of promise,
Which is the earnest of our inheritance until the redemption of the purchased possession, unto the praise of his glory."
Eph. 1:13 (KJV)

"The Lord is not slack concerning his promise, as some men count slackness; but is longsuffering to us-word, not willing that any should perish, but that all should come to repentance."
II Pet. 3:9 (KJV)

"Now thanks be unto God, which always causeth us to triumph in Christ, and maketh manifest the savour of his knowledge by us in every place.
For we are unto God a sweet savour of Christ, in them that are saved, and in them that perish:

To the one we are the savour of death unto death; and to the other the savour of life unto life. And who is sufficient for these things?

For we are not as many, which corrupt the word of God: but as of sincerity, but as of God, in the sight of God speak we in Christ."

II Cor. 2:14-17 (KJV)

"And he said unto me, My grace is sufficient for thee: for my strength is made perfect in weakness. Most gladly therefore will I rather glory in my infirmities, that the power of Christ may rest upon me."

II Cor. 12:9 (KJV)

Learning the scriptures is a lifelong journey. It's like a giant puzzle. When you're doing a puzzle, and all the pieces are there in front of you, you can only fit those pieces together that you can see; one at a time. All the other pieces remain until you get around to seeing where they fit. You have strategies and methods: such as color grouping, grouping of structures, and people, items, and shapes. As the pieces come together you find that if you have to force a piece to fit it probably doesn't belong there, so you must set it aside and wait until you find the right place for that piece within the puzzle. Sometimes you can accidentally, or stubbornly, leave the piece joined forcedly in place, thus making the full picture incorrect: of course, this will become evident in the end. Also, you can get pieces that seem to fit but are so closely dissimilar. These pieces are deceptive for the duration of the puzzle, but will be detected in the end when finally confronted with the genuine piece that fits.

There are countless spiritual leaders within the church who have established their interpretation of God's Truth by forcing the pieces to fit. I have learned through the years that in understanding God's word I must wait upon Him to guide me to the answers through prayer, studying, and meditation under the submission to His Holy Spirit. I am okay with not knowing something. I am okay if there appears to be a contradiction, because I know there are no contradictions in God's Truth, and it's just me not understanding; so, I wait until He makes it clear and he always does in His time. I am still waiting for clarity on some things.

Rest in Jesus.

"For we know in part, and we prophesy in part.

But when that which is perfect is come, then that which is in part shall be done away.

When I was a child, I spake as a child, I understood as a child, I thought as a child: but when I became a man, I put away childish things.

For now we see through a glass, darkly; but then face to face: now I know in part; but then shall I know even as also I am known.

And now abideth faith, hope, charity, these three; but the greatest of these is charity."

I Cor. 13:9-13 (KJV)

The failure of our spiritual leaders to rightly divide the Word of Truth has led countless sheep to the slaughter. Their misleading views have laid a path for compromise, conflict, confusion, worldliness, and sexual depravity. These leaders I'm referring to do not know Christ but use Him as a platform to achieve their own carnal desires. Mixed in with the wheat are the tares. They have drawn millions of souls away from the Truth and are partially responsible for the spiritual decay in our nation's congregations at present. These are those who have allowed homosexuality, transgenderism, sexual abuse, and pedophilia to enter into the congregations of our nation under the name of God. These are those who have promised salvation by means other than the way of the cross. This generation; being spiritually compromised by false doctrine; can only erode even further, for sin can only take its natural course when untethered, and only Truth can tether sin: so, being that Truth is in the process of being redefined by an insolent generation, what remains to stop the onslaught of sin? Only faith and repentance!

We know what the consequences shall be as Jesus describes in detail the spiritual condition of man in Mat. 24 and II Tim. 3

Even though divisions are possible in man's church, they are not possible in Christ's church: for in Christ's church all souls are resonated in Jesus by faith in Him for the forgiveness of sins: an indivisible bond congealed by the blood of Christ, and it is this Church that coexists with man's religions, and it is this Church that this nation is "Falling Away" from.

"Jesus answered them, I told you, and ye believed not: the works that I do in my Father's name, they bear witness of me.

But ye believed not, because ye are not my sheep, as I said unto you.

My sheep hear my voice, and I know them, and they follow me:

And I give unto them eternal life; and they shall never perish, neither shall any man pluck them out of my hand.

My Father, which gave them me, is greater than all; and no man is able to pluck them out of my Father's hand.

I and my Father are one."

Jn. 10:25-30 (KJV)

Interpreting the scripture is contingent upon our relationship with God through Jesus Christ. The more we submit ourselves to the Holy Spirit, and immerse ourselves in His Word, the more the Holy Spirit is able to enable us to rightly divide the Word of Truth.

CHAPTER 4

LOVE, LOVE, LOVE

"For, brethren, ye have been called unto liberty; only use not liberty for an occasion to the flesh, but by love serve one another.

For the law is fulfilled in one word, even in this; Thou shalt love thy neighbor as thyself.

But if ye bite and devour one another, take heed that ye be not consumed one of another."

Gal. 5:13-15

Love: the very core of God's character; but God's love and man's love are two different things. Because man is tainted, so is his love, but even still this love plays into every aspect of our lives, and the lack of it plays a critical role in the "Falling Away".

For the Christians, God's love dwells within them by the presence of the Holy Spirit. This is the love God wishes for us to radiate; a pure love; satisfying and sufficient. Man's attempt at love, without God, is the opposite.

In Mt 24:12 Jesus depicts man's spiritual decay at the time of the "Falling Away".

"And because iniquity shall abound, the love of many shall wax cold.

Mt. 24:12 (KJV)

When I hear the word "wax" I think of a candle—and our nation's candle is going out.

The word "iniquity" is used in the K.J.V. 276 times.

In both Greek and Hebrew, it is defined as meaning: wrongdoing, lawlessness, wickedness, perverseness, unrighteousness, sin.

So, it is all this that will abound to the point of extinguishing the love in the souls of many.

A world without "love". Imagine that!

Wickedness running rampant throughout our nation; pressing us to make decisions in order to survive; decisions we normally would not consider.

Killing, murder, sexual deviance, destruction, thievery, hatred, fire, chaos, lawlessness: engulfed in sin you can trust no one; you can love no one. You either become like them or die.

Christians will be forced to flee to survive or die in conflict. Will you be able to continue in love while your friends and family fall victim to the "Fallen" society around you? Will you be able to love your enemies? Your own family members will rise up against you in order to save their own skins.

Compromise is not an option; you can no longer ride the fence. You must choose a side, the iniquity of the masses or the love of God. Your heart will be forced to make the choice, and many will cave to oppression. Many will "Fall Away".

Today I see love still thriving around me. Everywhere I go the goodness in people radiates as we make the effort to love; but there is an anxiety in the air. Those abounding in sin are banding together to gratify their transgressions. By conducting large social movements, swaying political views, and organizing communities; these "fallen" are gaining power and are encroaching upon our nation in great numbers bringing to life the prophecy of "sin abounding".

Because the majority of our nation has ceased to exercise Godly values in our homes and in our government; we are now reaping the consequences of our decisions. The abuse of technology, a worldwide pandemic, and established immorality has sent our nation spiraling out of orbit. We now stand turned away from the spiritual theme of God as we consume the pleasures and riches of our world in unbridled fashion. Again I refer to II Tim. 3:1-9.

"This know also, that in the last days perilous times shall come.

For men shall be lovers of their own selves, covetous, boasters, proud, blasphemers, disobedient to parents, unthankful, unholy,

Without natural affection, trucebreakers, false accusers, incontinent, fierce, despisers of those that are good,

Traitors, heady, high minded, lovers of pleasure more than lovers of God;

Having a form of godliness, but denying the power thereof: from such turn away.

For of this sort are they which creep into houses and lead captive silly women laden with sins, led away with divers lusts,

Ever learning, and never able to come to the knowledge of the truth.

Now as Jannes and Jambres withstood Moses, so do these also resist the truth: men of corrupt minds, reprobate concerning the faith.

But they shall proceed no further: for their folly shall be manifest unto all men, as theirs also was."

II Tim. 3:1-9 (KJV)

It pangs me to see homosexuality accepted as normal human behavior; transgenderism being taught to our children; and the twisted rationale of our institutions supporting these perversions to fatten their own pockets. This is a deviance towards God's natural law. God did not create two men in the garden. He created man first and woman for a companion; we Christians know this; but iniquity does not. Sin cannot, and will not, accept the ways of God. That's why it's sin: the opposite of God's way. This sin is capable of justifying itself by rationalization and denial, making everything OK.

It was Shakespeare who said, "To thine own self be true". Our problems lie deep in our souls. They lay in a place that defies admonition, and in order to expose them we must bring them to light. There we will find ourselves face down before God confessing our transgressions and seeking His love and forgiveness; but then this has always been the problem with man; unable to face his sin: so, consequently drowning in it. This chapter is about love; but really; in relation to the "Falling Away"; it is about the lack of it.

"And then many shall be offended, and shall betray one another, and shall hate one another."
Mt. 24:10 (KJV)

The word "offend" means to trip up, to entice, to sin, apostasy, to be caused to offend.

Because society will fall so far from the face of God it will now be in the grip of evil. With the love in man quenched, hate will rise to the occasion.

THE MONSTER WITHIN

I hide behind
The corners in your mind.
No matter how hard you try:
My shadow you won't find.

Giving off no scent:
Revealing no signs:
Immune to the light:
To love I am blind.

Within the unusual man,
Who is larger than life:
I seek his soul
In the darkness of night.

Aware that I'm there:
He keeps me chained.
If not for love:
I would drive him insane.

Destroy me he would:
If he only could:
But I am part of his soul:
Though I'm no good.

So feed me! I cry:
For I'm always here.
I'm the monster within:
The father of fear.

I claw and I tear,
To break him down:
And seek to capitalize,
While he lays on the ground.

But the shield that he has:
It's made of "Immortal".
And I cannot defeat,
Or break through the forged portal.

I'll always be trapped here:
Until the day he dies:
And then be released:
To hear the great cries

Of the monsters before me:
Who shared the same fate.
I am the "Monster Within":
A.K.A. --- HATE.

Hatred has reared its ugly head and is immobilizing our communities from the major cities to the peaceful rural towns. Its effect is producing numerous and shocking acts of violence in our streets and in our schools. It has graduated from "going postal" to "killing children". As crime rises, the racial tension mounts: hatred fuels the fires of violence sweeping our nation. It's in our music, our movies, our books. It's on the news, on the street, on the bus. It's in our homes, in our schools, and in our government. It's in the souls of our people. We cry: "Where does it come from; all this hate? I've never seen hate like this before!".

It comes from the lack of love, and the lack of love comes from the lack of God, Jesus in particular. Where there is no light there is only darkness.

At the time of the "Falling Away" sin will evolve to such a magnitude that even God will judge the many by sending strong delusion, reinforcing their belief in the deceit they are entangled in.

"And with all deceivableness of unrighteousness in them that perish; because they received not the love of the truth, that they might be saved.

And for this cause God shall send them strong delusion, that they should believe a lie:"

II Thes. 2:10-11 (KJV)

With the love in people quenched, hate will rise to the occasion, and society will fall deep into the grip of evil. What we are witnessing in our nation presently is just a taste of what's to come.

We need to recognize *Rev. 13:10*

"He that leadeth into captivity shall go into captivity: he the killeth with the sword must be killed with the sword. Here is the patience and the faith of the saints."

Take an empty glass and leave it outside, undisturbed, for three months. It has no other option but to become filled with filth, moss, or stagnant rainwater, or it may evaporate.

Take the same glass and each day for three months fill it with clear drinking water. Add one drop of bleach. The glass will remain clean.

We must strive to keep our glasses filled with love.

Love. That so familiar word; expressed by so many different means: such as by poetry, music, sex, television, books and magazines.

Love. That so familiar word; expressed in so many different ways.

Love is a battleground.

Love is a seed waiting to blossom.

Love is a diamond.

Love is a kiss.

Love is forever.

Love is a puppy.

Love is pain.
Love is a mystery.
Love is caring.
Love is understanding.
Love is blind.
Love is God
Love is being together.
Love is trust.
Love is sacrifice.

And on and on we go!

You can ask 10 people the question: "What is love?"; And you can get 10 different answers. The word is synonymous with so many different meanings.

Webster defines "love" in the following ways.

● A deep and tender feeling of affection or devotion to a person or persons.

● An expression of one's love or affection.

● A feeling of brotherhood and goodwill towards other people.

● A strong liking for or interest in something.

● A strong, usually passionate affection of one person to another, based in part on sexual attraction.

● Sexual passion.

● Play for love i.e., play for nothing, tennis a score of zero.

● God's tender regard and concern for all human beings; devotion to and desire for God as the supreme God that all human beings have.

● Love implies intense fondness or deep devotion and may apply to various relationships or objects.

In the "Falling Away" most of these attributes will wax cold.

God's love will never grow cold towards man, but man's love will grow cold towards God and thus towards himself.

Love is the total essence of God bundled up in one word that man is incapable of achieving on his own.

This is the love that will wax cold. This is the love that is dying in our nation: the essence of God in man.

CHAPTER 5

LAODICEAN

"I know thy works, that thou art neither cold nor hot: I would thou wert cold or hot. So then because thou art luke-warm, and neither cold nor hot, I will spew thee out of my mouth."

Rev. 3:15-16 (KJV)

The profile of the Laodicean church is consistent with modern day churches within our nation, and throughout the world; and so are the profiles of the other six churches Jesus addressed.

Jesus' letters to the seven churches are written in such a manner as to portray Jesus as an all-seeing Shepherd looking over His newborn flock. He sees all through His just, loving, and truthful eyes: just as He did in the beginning with Adam and Eve. There is nowhere to run, nowhere to hide. He is telling His Church that He views into their souls and comprehends their true actions and motives that generate their works. Jesus knows your heart better than you do. He knows who is sincere and who is deceitful, who is incapable of sincerity, and who desires the truth. In the case of the Laodicean church, He sees their blindness, self-righteousness, hypocrisy, and indifference.

Jesus uses water temperature to describe the spiritual condition of His church at Laodicea. The temperature represents the condition of their souls which is evident by their works, actions, and deeds.

"Enter ye in at the straight gate: for wide is the gate, and broad is the way, that leadeth to destruction, and many there be which go in thereat:

Because straight is the gate, and narrow is the way, which leadeth unto life, and few there be that find it.

Beware of false prophets, which come to you in sheep's clothing, but inwardly they are ravening wolves.

Ye shall know them by their fruits. Do men gather grapes or thorns, or figs of thistles?

Even so every good tree bringeth forth good fruit; but a corrupt tree bringeth forth evil fruit.

A good tree cannot bring forth evil fruit, neither can a corrupt tree bring forth good fruit.

Every tree that bringeth not forth good fruit is hewn down, and cast into the fire.

Wherefore by their fruits ye shall know them."

Mt. 7:13-20 (KJV)

All seven churches were geographically located in an area, Asia Minor, just north of the Mediterranean Sea. It stands to reason that some of these letters-if not all-were passed around to each of the churches. Col. 4:16 Indicates this possibility. The seven churches were being assaulted by satan by way of existing religious sects, satanic worship, false gods, cults, and the Nicolaitans.

Jesus is specific in his praises and rebukes, and in the case of the Laodicean church, only a rebuke.

What is so powerful that it can take a "HOT" New Testament church, on fire for Jesus, and bring it to a lost and fallen state in 45 years? It's a simple answer. Sin!

As we see in Matthew, the broad path of destruction: sin, comes in many forms. It is the specific combination of sins that placed the Laodicean church into a near hopeless condition, a lukewarm condition. The church has evolved into a state of apathy, indifference, self-righteousness, and blindness, no longer conscious of the need for God as their provider for everyday life and salvation. Within just a few generations it has fallen back from a church established in Christ to a church established in itself: thus, providing no spiritual fruit and no genuine conversions.

Too many churches in our nation have followed this same path. Their pews are filled with dead souls; live and vibrant; cheerful about their way; fat in their own luxury; comfortable in their apostasy.

Lukewarm is a term often used in describing water. The water is undesirable, tepid, distasteful, and unless you are in a dire situation, such as dying of thirst; the water is useless, and often spilled to the ground. Lukewarm also represents a middle ground; an in between hot and cold; a mixture. Lukewarm water originates by action. When hot and cold water combine the temperatures reach a compromising state.

Laodicea is a church that mutated into a generation of people who called themselves Christians because of their origin but lost their understanding of fellowship with Jesus the Savior. Poor leadership accompanied with misleading doctrine resulted in spiritual starvation for each generation in line. An abundance of wealth gave way to worldliness, resulting in indifference, self-righteousness, spiritual blindness, and material distraction. The Nicolaitans also had influence in producing immorality and a "Falling Away" from the understanding of grace.

In just a few generations this church backslid to the point of falling from grace: generations of children evolving further and further from the truth in a very short time.

"Christ is become of no effect unto you, whosoever of you are justified by the law; ye are fallen from grace."
Gal. 5:4 (KJV)

God's word repeatedly warns us of the potential consequences of wealth, and how it can consume us by its ability to satisfy every pleasure under the sun. Laodicea fell victim to this very thing. Their wealth left them confident in their earthly possessions, thus distracting them from their spiritual needs.

They became a church caught up in themselves and in their own vanities; lying to themselves and acting upon those lies. By a mixture of Christianity and sin they became hypocrites claiming to be one thing but exemplifying another. They carried the logo but did not provide the example. They advertised but did not deliver.

They had a form of godliness but denied the power thereof. They approached God on their own terms laying their own foundation for their salvation: by believing their own lie they could now claim entry into heaven; all the while not seeing their self-righteousness had left them blind and lost. They deceived themselves into believing their own riches and deeds could draw them close to God. They no longer approached God by His rules: humble and penitent through Jesus only. If they did so they would have initiated the beginning of a true spiritual relationship resulting in a powerful, victorious walk with the Father. They were most sickening because they claimed to be God-like, but they were secretly and openly most sinful; lacking the power within their soul to overcome and repent from their sin.

Place yourself in an underground basement with no windows; total darkness; pitch black. Open the basement door and the light enters. You were in a void where the light was absent, but upon opening the door the light entered, and became present, and now you can see. The moment you begin to reach for the knob is the moment you begin to believe. You know that when you open that door the light will enter. You're still in the dark and you can't see. You believe without seeing. Darkness is the absence of light and believing is more than seeing.

"Jesus saith unto him, Thomas, because thou hast seen me, thou hast believed: blessed are they that have not seen, and yet have believed."

Jn. 20:29 (KJV)

So many around me live in the basement and have not yet opened the door. They wander through their years never understanding or caring for their souls. They see with their eyes but not with their souls. They are detached from their souls. They have starved their souls willfully and have traded their souls for something degradable. They will not reach for the knob to open the door; for if they would, the Light would enter in, and they would see.

"Behold, I stand at the door, and knock: if any man hear my voice, and open the door, I will come into him, and will sup with him, and he with me."

Rev. 3:20 (KJV)

For those who understand the light, and experience it, know that it is supplied by God. We open that door and Jesus unites with our soul; illuminating it with His wisdom, generosity, and love; so, we can see how things really are; so, we can see the truth. The darkness fades and we find we are gradually transformed into a person with purpose, self-control, and wisdom.

We enjoy God's creation-and being a part of it; not needing much of anything else as He provides for us, and protects us, and prepares the paths that we choose as we live in His Light. We allow the Light in. We do not push it out, doubting it, mocking it, denying its existence.

Some say it is no coincidence that the Laodicean church is the last of the seven churches addressed by Jesus, and it also exemplifies the fallen characteristics of society in the last days. A society whose love is propelled by material values instead of spiritual values, such as caring, patience, and understanding. A society blind of spiritual substance; utterly lost in its own vanities and pleasures. A society detached from its very soul. A society producing a culmination of character defects that renders its people incapable of being truthful with themselves, resulting in spiritual blindness.

Pride will take the reins and pride cometh before the fall.

The difference between one who is physically blind and one who is spiritually blind is that the physically blind knows he is blind; the spiritually blind does not.

Until you clean the fishbowl the fish can't see that it has merely been going in circles.

THE COOLER

Mr. Red — "When I buy things, I expect them to be built to last a long, long time, and not break down in a few years."

Mr. Blue— "I already know that most things I buy are built not to last. I'm fortunate to find something that does, so I'll use it to its fullest, and get rid of it when it breaks, and then replace it with a new one."

Mr. Red and Mr. Blue were shopping one day for fishing gear, and they ran across a great deal on a cooler. Each man bought one.

Now, Mr. Red is meticulous with all his possessions; keeping them clean, oiled and dusted, in tiptop shape; so that when they age they will still look like new.

Mr. Blue could hardly care about his things because he knows as they age they begin to break down, and no matter how clean they look, they still don't work like they used to. For Blue, once something does not function as it did when it was new; if he can't fix it; he dumps it. For Red, he holds on, continuing to believe it's still working because he spent so much time cleaning it to keep it in working condition.

Well, after three years their coolers began to show signs of wear. Blue's cooler didn't want to seal tight and snappy like when it was new. Things didn't seem as cold as they used to be. Red's cooler; the same way; but Red insisted the drinks were still cold enough. His cooler still looked new, like the day he bought it. Blue's looked rough, beat up, and stained. Blue replaced his cooler with a new one and continued to enjoy ice cold beverages, while Red held onto his for years insisting his beverages were still cold. Why couldn't Red admit that his beverages weren't as cold as they used to be when his cooler was new?

Sometimes Blue would get a drink from Red's cooler and it would be lukewarm. He would spew it out.

Despite the fallen condition of the Laodicean church, Jesus always has room for the penitent heart. And He offers them hope and confirms His love; for we know that our Father is longsuffering towards His creation and is not willing that any should perish, but that all would come to repentance.

"The Lord is not slack concerning his promise, as some men count slackness; but is longsuffering to us-ward, not willing that any should perish, but that all should come to repentance."
II Pet. 3:9 (KJV)

Failure to repent can bring disastrous consequences. Read your Bible! Look at Cain, the people of Noah's time, the Israelites, and pharaoh.

On the other hand, the act of repentance brings God's mercy. See Jonah 3:5-10

Failure to repent brings eternal separation and the judgment of God. If you don't budge, God will judge.

Judgment is contingent upon repentance, and if you are sincere that repentance occurs simultaneously when you place faith in Jesus Christ as your savior and Lord. When you call upon Him for forgiveness of sin you make evident your genuine sorrow for your sinful state by turning away from sin and turning toward the way of Jesus. You see the sacrifice He has made for you, and the cost of your salvation, and you can no longer travel that road of sin which Jesus suffered to defeat, to forgive, to atone for. You now struggle and fight against sin.

Before you embraced it, lavishing its pleasures; beckoning to its every whim; a slave to your very nature.

In our nation today sin advances upon us in all its forms. Violence, depravity, apostasy, hypocrisy, faithlessness, betrayal, deceit, drugs, riots, mass murders, homosexuality, transgenderism, human trafficking, humanism, false teachings, blindness, self-righteousness, unconstrained sexual behavior, pornography, pedophilia, devil worship, materialism, worldliness, atheism, etc.

As sin advances around us we must rise to the occasion by defending Truth. We must become louder, not timid. We must find courage, not cowardice. We must put on the armor of God and not take it off.

THE AJAX OF FAITH

Ajax — A great Athenian warrior in the time of Troy who wielded a giant hammer.

I visualize Ajax as a great champion standing up on a hill, cutting down the enemy man after man. This battle continues day after day, and this battle is similar to mine as I learn to die daily for the cause of Christ.

My slain self piles up.
My flesh never ceases to press upon me.
I beat it back.
I tire.

When does it end?

"O wretched man that I am! Who shall deliver me from the body of this death?
I thank God through Jesus Christ our Lord. So then with the mind I myself serve the law of God; but with the flesh the law of sin."
Rom. 7:24-25 (KJV)

I look into my life's past; standing now on a mountain of sin defeated.

Sins cut down in battle:
Sins forgiven:
Sins defeated:
Sins erased.

Upon this mountain a champion:
Victorious in battle as I swing the long Sword of the Spirit.
I stand before the onslaught of sin.
I have not yet perfected the wearing of this armor.
Nicks and cuts appear upon my soul.
Sin briefly penetrates but cannot break through.
I bleed, but not unto death!
Scars are evident from sins past healed.
I would die in the heat of this battle if not for
The armor which fuels me, heals me,
Strengthens me, protects me.

My faith in the Blood brings forgiveness and stops the bleeding.

My faith in prayer keeps my soul in contact with the throne and heals the wounds.

My faith in this armor strengthens me and protects my entire soul.

Oh this armor of grace; presented to me by my Lord Jesus Christ.

The helmet assures me that He will never leave me nor forsake me.

The sword slashes back as I speak its Word; believing what I utter.

My loincloth is tempered with the Truth so I will not follow a lie.

My chest is protected by the presence of Jesus, who has transformed me into the warrior that I am.

My boots are broken in by the years of studying the Word, so as to keep me balanced, so I will not fall.

I gaze across the battlefield, and I see my brothers. They swing away; battle worn; battle tired; battle scarred.

I gaze to the horizon: an endless sea of sin: and I remember.

"And when he had opened the fifth seal, I saw under the altar the souls of them that were slain for the word of God, and for the testimony which they held:

And they cried with a loud voice, saying, "How long, O Lord, holy and true, dost thou not judge and avenge our blood on them that dwell on the earth?"

Rev. 6:9-10 (KJV)

Shelter me oh God from this onslaught of sin, for I am tired and weary.

"Plead my cause, O Lord, with them that strive with me: fight against them that fight against me.

Take hold of shield and buckler, and stand up for mine help.

Draw out also the spear, and stop the way against them that persecute me: say unto my soul, I am thy salvation."
Ps. 35:1-3 (KJV)

He strengthens me to continue the fight; for I, like my brothers, am an Ajax of Faith; a champion victorious, upon the mountain of sin, by the grace of my Lord Jesus Christ.

"I can do all things through Christ which strengtheneth me."
Phil. 4:13 (KJV)

"Finally, my brethren, be strong in the Lord, and in the power of his might.
Put on the whole armor of God, that ye may be able to stand against the wiles of the devil.
For we wrestle not against flesh and blood, but against principalities, against powers, against the rulers of the darkness of this world, against spiritual wickedness in high places.
Wherefore take unto you the whole armor of God, that ye may be able to withstand in the evil day, and having done all, to stand.
Stand therefore, having your loins girt about with truth, and having on the breastplate of righteousness;
And your feet shod with the preparation of the gospel of peace;

Above all, taking the shield of faith, wherewith ye shall be able to quench all the fiery darts of the wicked.

And take the helmet of salvation, and the sword of the Spirit, which is the word of God:

Praying always with all prayer and supplication in the Spirit, and watching thereunto with all perseverance and supplication for all saints;"

Eph. 6:10-18 (KJV)

CHAPTER 6

THINGS TO PONDER

"Fools multiply when wise men are silent."

Nelson Mandela

Faith touches God.

It's not complicated. There is light and there is darkness. There is light during the day, and dark during the night. There is light and darkness that exists within the souls of men. You either follow the light or you follow the dark. All the rest is a mere consequence resulting from this choice. Which one do you follow?

We are a Tower of Babel: constantly pressing upward in pride and arrogance; never satisfied; pushing headlong until we crumble and fall. Our technology is evolving in such a manner. It is advancing out of control, and we refuse to see it. What we intended to be useful and efficient is turning out to be destructive and chaotic. A great depression is coming as a consequence of failing to balance our technology.

Just as the Supreme Court saw fit to reduce the spiritual pulse of our nation, it is now time for them to revive the heartbeat before we suffer a stroke that we cannot recover from.

WHAT AM I ?

I've loved you since the day you were born.
I have watched you grow; year after year; into the
wonderful person you are now.
It hurts me when you take things out on me,
or ignore me because I'm right.
Yah! I know. "I'm always right!"
Well can I help it if I am?
It's quite a burden being right all the time.
You ought to know!
I deserve respect! That's right! RESPECT!
I need attention too. Like everyone else, I need to be
talked to, embraced, and loved.

I need to be heard, listened to, and understood.
I need you to sacrifice some of your precious time,
and sit with me a while, and for once listen to what
I have to say.
And don't you dare be getting angry with me,
and start tossing me around, and not communicate
with me for days.
Of course, I hope you'll never lock me in the closet.
Talk about trauma!
Please promise me you'll always love me and never leave me,
for I promise you the same
and together we'll grow old and prosper, and love.

THEOS LOGOS

Filter the quarry of complexity into a thimble of simplicity.

It's amazing how much faith man can place on fleeing from Earth to Mars. If man can't master his faith on earth; what makes him think he can master himself on Mars?

Man is destroying the planet he has been given and now he wants a second chance; yet concerning his faith, he cannot see it is his lack of faith that brings his destruction: a faith misplaced. Now he drags the same burden of sin from Earth to Mars. Does he still not believe in the Creator? The same God who created Earth created Mars. Look at man as he defies the obvious while he searches for the obscure; learning nothing from his mistakes; still drowning in his intellectual pride. Watch him run like a child invisible and indestructible. What will he do when his Creator finally appears? Will his state of denial increase, or will he humble himself to the Truth? Oh, these men who think that if a tree falls in the forest, and no one is there to hear it, it won't make a sound because they choose to believe it won't. Maybe it's about time they should hear the sound that the tree makes.

Time travel has been around way before Einstein discovered its potential truth with E=mc /squared: the theory of relativity. Truth in fact; God created it. You say, "that's a little crazy". No one has gone forward or backward in time. Einstein concluded that mass (m) and kinetic energy (E) are equal since the speed of light is constant. Therefore, mass can be changed into energy and energy into mass.

Each of us is born with a soul. From the moment of conception, we begin our travel through time; or I'd rather say "eternity". We are living in eternity right now. Time is a system of measurement created by God in the form of a day so we can measure our existence at a constant speed during our lifetime. Eternity is timeless; although there probably is a measurement to determine how long it takes to get from point A to point B: let's describe that as being "an instant". There is no beginning or end in eternal life therefore there is no need for time. God existed infinitely before our existence and will do so after our existence. You existing with Him is your purpose; or will you exist without Him? Those of us who receive His gift are promised eternal life with Him in eternity. Those who reject Him are promised eternal separation in the lake of fire. So, for the "lost" life is limited to a short existence here on earth; measured by time; that briefly brushes the vast space of eternity there in heaven, where we who are saved are now allowed to share eternity because of the shed blood of Jesus. I now suggest to you God's formula for relativity, and it is no theory.

$$E=JC^3$$

(E) being eternity; (J) being Jesus; (C) being Christ; and (3 or cubed)

being The Father, The Son, and the Holy Spirit.

Webster defines "relative" as: dependent upon or referring to each other. A person connected to another by blood, marriage or kinship.

Jesus did all this for man when He changed His energy into mass, and became man, and then changed from man back into energy, and returned to His rightful place at the right hand of God as a representative for all individuals who will believe Him to be "The Way, The Truth, and the Life".

Relativity? —The Father, the Son, and the Holy Spirit are the most relative presence in existence. They have connected us by blood, joined us through marriage, and forged an eternal kinship, unbreakable through eternity.

If you don't believe God can move a mountain, then you need to get out of the pulpit.

I heard a man once say; "I hope that we all have not deluded ourselves into thinking we are saved and are going to heaven". My response – There is no delusion in the faith of the blood of our Lord Jesus.

We have millions of Christians studying the Word of God who are not at the throne. What do you think they are going to walk away with?

Our nation is spiritually sick. Continue to feed your body the wrong foods for decades and you will eventually pay the price for your apathy and lack of discipline. We have been living on a diet of depravity, drunkenness, drugs, denial, depression and deception. Looks like we get a "D" for a grade and if things don't change, we'll get an "F" for "Fallen".

We are the "UFOs". We are the unidentified flying objects. Cave wall paintings, hieroglyphics, ancient alphabets on stone tablets; all indicating extraterrestrial life: all products of an overactive imagination of creative thinkers of that day. Artists relaying their imagination on stone. We of this day in time have the same habits, and yet we think that because we find these ancient symbols that they mean "ET" visited this planet way back then. So, before you know it, we've imagined ourselves right out of believing the proven truth that God is our Creator, and all life revolves around all that is true about Him. Anything to distract us from this fact; to lead us astray, to confuse the issue of Truth. We look out into space for the answers to life when the answers are right there in front of us. We are life. We are the answer. We are the UFOs, flying through eternal space, through this present time, unidentified in our own personal identity crisis. Who are we? We are members of God's creation; adrift on an ocean of deception; because we can't see the Truth of God laid out before us.

I could go on and discuss definitions of pre-trib, post–trib, and millennial; but I choose not to ruffle your feathers. There's a lot of chickens in the coop and a lot of feathers flying in the air. I'll just let the wind carry the feathers where it will.

You can refuse to acknowledge the Truth and yet that in itself is acknowledgement.

The question is: "What is it that drives a person to seek righteousness?". Moreover, "What is it that prevents that person from finding it?". A need for forgiveness? Absolution of guilt?

A veil over the ugly evil that lies within us? Are we taught to be "good" contrary to our sinful nature?

It's true when you receive Jesus into your heart the Holy Spirit begins to guide and direct you towards holiness, therefore any righteousness we display is a result of God working in our heart, and not of our own making, yet it is of our own choosing. Many souls will seek righteousness and desire to be accounted as good and acceptable before God. Righteousness without Jesus is unacceptable and unattainable; for within a person's soul there exists unrighteousness; or sin. Sin casts a blemish upon us that we cannot conceal. Jesus was unblemished as a pure lamb and sacrificed for us; thus, covering our unrighteousness before God. It's your faith in Jesus' sacrifice that brings us righteousness and allows us to stand righteous before God, in the righteousness of His Son. So, one seeking to be righteous outside of God is self-righteous and it is this reflection a person sees in himself that blinds him from seeing the Truth.

THE BROKEN MILE

By Fred Hussey

Take my hand and don't let go.
As we seek to reach that destined place:
Where champions glow, and victories echo
Down the narrow aisle, for those who suffered
The broken mile.

That broken mile: when all has failed
Except the well laid course of traps and lies.
Where relations die along with your smile,
And the only goodness is in your child,
As despair becomes your faithful friend,
Drawing you to an early end.

Take the heart of this glorious child:
Your future, your hope, your only song.
Do not fall and do not crawl,
But stand tall and fake the smile:
While you trudge this broken mile.

You can't lay down, and you can't give up.
You can't allow your only song,
To become involved; for this trip is long,
And if it does, you'll most likely fade:
As you hear the screams of your broken child,
In the grips of this relentless mile.

This broken mile
Is the point in time:
Where do or die,
Are not just rhyme,
But all is tested in this arena,

Where the best are bested,
And the "all togethers"
Are helpless screamers.
Insanity raining in an ironic play,
And all become strange,
In the dark of day.

If you have no child to lean upon:
Then you'll most likely fall, a broken pawn:
Lest you look to God for ends relief:
For newly strength to quench the grief:
That has sorely consumed your tired heart,

And in the Almighty you'll find the Child:
Who walked this mile years before:
Who suffered and died to become a door:
For us to enter into the distant place:
Where champions glow and victories echo; down a
Narrow aisle for those who suffered the broken mile.

April 16, 2001

Our nation is in bed with sin. It is asleep, but this is no dream. Can we awaken; or have we reached the point of coma?

Whenever God had to step in and judge man it was not pretty: extremely harsh, no mercy, no leniency. It seems the leniency is shown in the time before His patience runs out, or at the time of repentance. We are in the time of leniency.

The "deviled egg"! Once you start eating them it's hard to stop.

CHAPTER 7

SOLUTION

"If my people, which are called by my name, shall humble themselves, and pray, and seek my face, and turn from their wicked way; then will I hear from heaven, and will forgive their sin, and will heal their land."

II Chr. 7:14 (KJV)

PROLOGUE

ME'-NE, ME'-NE, TE'-KEL, U-PHAR'-SIN.
numbered, numbered, weighed, divided.

Dan. 5:25 (KJV)